TABLE OF CONTENTS

MW00389890

Foreword

This book is for you if:

- Sewing is not your strong point or you don't have a machine.
- You've recently moved and need some quick and easy window solutions.
- You're looking for economical, temporary treatments for a baby or child's room.
- You love creative, one-of-a-kind looks in hardware, tie-backs and valances.
- You prefer to do it yourself, or have a limited budget.

We offer the solutions you're looking for: dozens of creative, custom window ideas with an emphasis on ease and economy. Most of the beautiful window treatments on these pages can be put together in minutes, and no-sewing is required!

In this book, you'll learn how to take advantage of easy fabric adhesives and ready-made trims and accessories to alter fabric pieces and purchased panels. Included are tips to create unique hardware and tiebacks.

Before you begin any of the following projects, refer to the General Instructions starting on page 92 to familiarize yourself with no-sew techniques. Then:

1. choose the treatment you want to make
2. select your fabric
3. choose hardware
4. measure windows (see page 92)
5. install hardware
6. figure how much fabric you'll need (see page 94)
7. cut fabric and make the treatment.
8. hang it up

FABULOUS FABRICS

LONDON SHADE

This graceful variation on a classic roman shade is the height of sophisticated window dressing. Yet, you can easily achieve this beautiful designer look without paying a designer price, and you don't even have to get out a sewing machine! The fabric hem and rod casing is formed with fusing tape or glue, and tie-on silk cording creates the pretty shape. (What a great substitute for the complicated ring cords usually used for these shades.)

Supplies:

Floral fabric (Waverly Fabrics)

Ivory cord

Fusing tape or fabric glue

Spring-tension rod

4

1. Measure the window and cut length of fabric to allow for hems and casing. Add an extra 3" to the width to allow for hems and slight gathering.

2. Hem fabric on three sides.

3. Create a casing at the top using either fusing tape or fabric glue.

4. Thread casing onto the rod.

5. Cut two strips of cord to desired length (ours were about 40" each, but this will depend on the size of the window). Fold cord over the top of rod and tie at the bottom of shade (in about 9" on each side). Fan-fold fabric on either side and press with your fingers. Allow the cords to hang down a bit.

6. Tie the ends in a knot and fringe.

VINTAGE CLOTH

If you love a retro look in the kitchen, don't leave your windows out of the loop. Many stores carry reproduction tablecloth fabrics reminiscent of the charming patterns found in the 1940s and '50s.

This look was created with printed fabric panels, the scalloped valance of coordinating oilcloth (also a throwback to a bygone era.) No-sew hem and casing techniques make this project quick and easy. Wouldn't grandma have loved that?

Supplies:

Reproduction vintage fabric with fruit pattern

Red-and-white check oilcloth

Cup and marking pen or pencil

Fusing tape or fabric glue

Spring-tension rod

Decorative pole rod

1. For curtains: Make two panels of fabric to fit window. Multiply window measurement by 1½ to allow for gathers. Iron in the casing and the hems. Then either glue them or use fusing tape to hem and create casing.

2. For valance: Cut the oilcloth to fit the width of the window and about 12" to 14" in length.

3. To make the scallops: On the wrong side of the oilcloth, use a cup or small dish as a guide and with a marking pen, trace half circles along the bottom edge of the cloth. Cut out the scallops using sharp scissors.

4. Staple the valance to the back of the pole rod and roll up as far as desired and staple again at the back.

5. Slip the curtains over the spring-tension rod.

Idea

Use a 1½" diameter unfinished dowel as an alternative to using a decorative rod. Novelty wood pieces from a craft or home improvement center can be decorated and used for finials.

A vintage tablecloth may also be used for this treatment. Search flea markets or garage sales for these colorful and nostalgic treasures.

TOILE BALLOON SHADE

It's hard to believe, but this perfectly shaped balloon shade is formed without taking a stitch with needle and thread. Iron-on shirring tape works the magic, gathering fabric with the tug of a string. The hems and rod casing come courtesy of fabric glue, so the whole project's no-sew easy. The hardest part is also the most fun—choosing just the right fabrics to decorate your windows!

Supplies

Toile fabric (Waverly)

Double-cord iron-on shirring tape

Fusing tape or fabric glue

Spring-tension rod

1. Measure window and cut fabric width an extra 3" to allow for hems and slight gathering from tape treatment. Cut the length to allow for casing and hem. Hem the fabric on three sides using the fusing tape or fabric glue.

2. Create a casing at the top edge of the fabric to fit the rod.

3. Cut four strips of the shirring tape into strips one third the length of the finished curtain.

4. On the back of the panel and starting about 2½" up from the bottom, iron a strip to each edge of the fabric. Iron the other two strips evenly spaced between these two.

5. Tie the cords in knots at the top of the shirring tape.

6. Hang the curtain on the rod and start pulling the cords to form gathers, arranging poufs in the shade. Tie the cords in knots at the bottom to secure. Stuff with tissue paper if desired to maintain shape.

Supplies:
Sheer fabric (preferably with stripes)
Strings of sequins, assorted colors
Fabric glue
Fusing tape
Curtain rod

1. Measure window and cut fabric width an extra 3" to allow for hems and slight gathering. Cut the length to allow for casing and hem.

2. Iron in the hems and casing. Hem sides and bottom using fabric glue or fusing tape.

3. Create the casing to fit the rod size, using fusing tape or fabric glue.

4. Cut the sequin strands different lengths and place on the fabric to decide your arrangement. Pin the strands once you're happy with the arrangement.

5. Place a yardstick or long piece of cardboard in the casing while gluing on the sequins so that you don't glue the casing closed. Move it frequently so that it doesn't get stuck in the casing. Following the stripe of the fabric, glue the sequin strands to the panel.

6. Slip the panel over the rod.

Idea

Besides using sequins for this treatment, ribbon or other interesting trims could be used. A walk down the aisle of the trims and ribbon section of your local fabric or craft store will reveal a vast array of choices. You might even want to mix and match ribbons with trim for an interesting arrangement.

SEQUINS FOR SHIMMER

Just right for a young "glamour girl," these sheer curtains are bedecked with sparkly sequins in a mix of jewel tones. Striped curtain fabric provides an easy guide to follow when gluing on the sequin strands, which vary in length for visual interest. With the curtain hems and casing done with no-sew fusing tape, this winning window treatment project couldn't be simpler!

FRAMED TEXTILES

If you think of a small, bare window as a frame, you might be inspired to create a work of art to fill it, painting a picture, of sorts, with textiles. This interesting display is done with taupe linen pieces cut into graduated shapes for layering. The pieces are hand-fringed and then attached together with attractive, silver grommets. Hanging in the center of the window from a spring rod and ribbon ties, this piece is a unique window treatment indeed.

Supplies:

Taupe linen

Medium silver grommets

Grommet kit

Black-and-white check ribbon, ¼" wide (about 2 yards per panel)

Spring-tension rod

1. Cut linen into three pieces (per panel) as follows, 5" x 5", 9" x 12", and 15" x 25". (Adjust these measurements to fit your particular window).

2. Fringe all edges of the three pieces about ½" in.

3. Attach the two smaller pieces to each other by affixing grommets (following grommet kit instructions) in each corner of the smallest piece (as pictured in photo). Pin both pieces to the large piece and affix with grommets in all four corners of the middle piece.

4. Affix grommets to the four corners of the large piece.

5. Cut ribbon into 20" lengths. Thread the ribbon through the top two grommets. Tie onto rod and trim tails. Then slip the ribbon over the rod.

☀ Idea

For an altogether different look for this treatment, try using cording or twine as hangers to replace the ribbons.

To keep fringe from raveling further, use a liquid fray preventative along the edge.

IVY ENTWINED

Pair a length of green, gauzy fabric with a garland of faux ivy and there you have it—instant swag to turn a needy window into a stunner. This soft, pretty look would coordinate well with today's natural home furnishing styles. The fabric drapes loosely around the rod, the ends cascading to the floor, or midway, depending on your preference. Add the garland, then stand back and admire your handiwork!

Supplies:

Green gauze fabric

Ivy garlands

Decorative pole rod

1. Measure length of window, then drape a measuring tape or piece of string across rod to measure for width. Wait to cut fabric until you've tried it on the rod.

2. Starting at one end of the rod, let fabric hang to desired length.

3. Then wrap fabric around the rod, draping as desired. Allow the other end to hang to desired length. The swag could be short or go all the way to the floor.

4. Wrap the ivy garland around the rod following the drape of the fabric.

MEADOW VIEW

This lushly pretty window treatment seems to come straight out of a trendy catalog, yet you can create it with very little time and money. Uneven edges are part of the charm of this filmy, yellow gauze fabric, so there isn't even a need for a hem. Faux blossoms are glued to the material, and also affixed to pushpins. Pinned up to a casual drape, this flowery panel will be a sure scene stealer!

Supplies:

Pale yellow gauze fabric (scrim)
Silk blossoms, colors of your choice
Pushpins
Fabric glue
Hot glue gun and glue sticks

1. Measure window. You will need enough fabric to allow for the draping.

2. Cut the fabric. Because of the nature of this fabric, no hems are needed.

3. Remove the backs from the silk blossoms and glue them randomly to the fabric using fabric glue.

4. Glue blossoms to the end of several pushpins using hot glue. Use the pushpins to hang the panel, draping it to give it a graceful look.

SILKY FRINGE

A beautiful silk fabric is only minutes away from its rightful place as the star of your bare window. Cut to the right size, it needs only to be altered with fusing tape or glue and hand-fringed for a striking curtain and fold-over valance. A few threads removed creates the pretty fringe, while the sides are hemmed. The casing is also created, and then you're ready to coordinate hardware for a gorgeous finish.

Supplies:

Plaid silk fabric

Fusing tape or fabric glue

Liquid fray preventative

Finial and rod (see page 81)

For this treatment you will need to use a woven fabric that is the same on both sides.

1. Measure and cut fabric. Multiply window measurement by 1½ to allow for gathers. Add 5" to the length for the top to overlap to the front.

2. Fringe the top and bottom edges. Use fray preventative along the fringed edges.

3. Use fabric glue to hem the edges (neatly as these will show on the front when turned over at the top for the valance).

4. With right side of fabric facing up, turn top of curtain down 3" or 4" and press with iron.

5. Open fabric back up and measure down and mark for casing (the casing should be wide enough to cover the rod).

6. Run a bead of fabric glue along the marked line. Fold fabric back down and press with fingers.

7. Thread the curtain over the rod.

2

EASY
EMBELLISHMENTS

PRETTY IN RIBBONS

It's pure pleasure to make your own curtains when you can skip the fabric fuss and go straight to the embellishment stage. Purchased pre-made from a fabric store, these violet sheers are pretty enough, but silver grommets and lush ribbon give them real custom flair. A handy kit helps you insert the grommets, then just thread the wire-edge ribbons through. The generous length of these unique tie-tops lends a languid, lovely look to this window

Supplies:

Purchased violet panels

Medium silver grommets

Grommet tools or kit

Craft knife

Coordinating wire edge ribbon, ¾" wide

Decorative pole rod

1. With a craft knife, make small slits in the top of the panel evenly spaced.

2. Attach grommets over the slits (following manufacturer's instructions).

3. Cut ribbon into 16" lengths and thread through each grommet.

4. Tie ribbons to the rod. Trim tails of ribbon if necessary.

♡ **Hint**

To mark sheer or other delicate fabric panels for grommet placement, use nonpermanent fabric markers or tailor's chalk.

SHOOTING STAR

Jewelry does wonders for a plain outfit, so why not a pair of sheer, white curtain panels? Hanging from starry-silver curtain hooks, these beaded wires gleam with colorful baubles that glisten in the sunlight. No two strands are exactly alike, and creating them is great fun for a beadwork lover. This arty window look is very today, and so eye-catching it's apt to be the focal point of the room!

Supplies:

Tie top panels

Assorted beads and colored wire

Needlenose pliers

Star drapery hooks and rod

1. Thread beads on wire. Hot glue them in position. Bend wire as pictured and create spirals at the end. Create a hook on the other end.

2. Tie the panels onto the drapery hooks.

3. Attach the wired bead strands by hooking them over the drapery hooks.

4. Slide the drapery hooks over the rod.

BETTER WITH BEADS

Draped across a rod to form a graceful swag, this purchased panel is so much more interesting with the added bead fringe. If you love to make beaded jewelry, this project is especially for you. Even novices can easily form these strands and attach them along the fabric edge. In gold, black and rust, the bead colors are chosen to match the curtain and hardware, creating an exquisitely coordinated window.

Supplies:

Purchased panel

Assorted beads - gold, black and rust

Wire and wire cutters

Needlenose pliers

1. Close one end of the wire and then thread the beads, 3 to 4 per strand. Leave the other end extending about 1" - 1½".

2. Add bead strands evenly spaced across one long end of the panel by piercing the fabric with the extended end of the wire. Push through and with needlenose pliers, twist the wire around the top of the beaded wire to secure.

3. Drape over the rod so that beads hang along the bottom edge of the panel and form a valance over the top.

ALL THE TRIMMINGS

There's no need to buy expensive curtains when a 10-minute procedure can transform an economical purchase. These solid color tab-tops are quite affordable and the added tapestry trim gives them upscale panache. A wide variety of beautiful trims are available in fabric stores, all quickly applied to curtains and drapes with fabric glue. For instant custom window treatments, what could be easier?

Supplies:

Purchased tab top panels

3" wide tapestry trim (Conso)

Fabric glue

Decorative pole rod

1. Cut the tapestry trim to fit the width of the curtains. Allow ½" on each side for turning.

2. Glue the trim along the top edge of the curtains. Fold one short edge of the trim to back of each side of the panel and glue. Allow to dry.

3. Slip the curtains over the rod.

3

FOR
THE KIDS

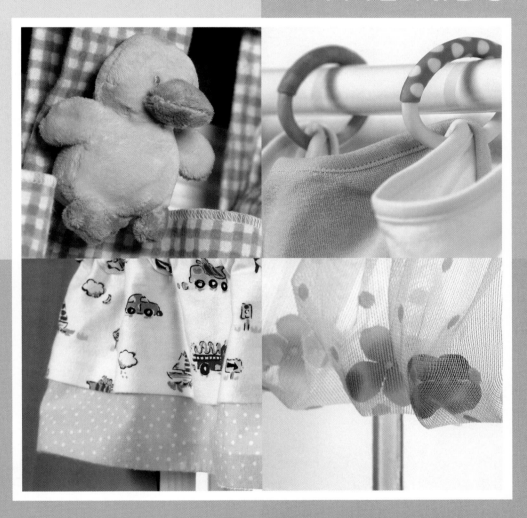

ZOO VIEW

Here's a baby's room look that's truly precious and definitely one-of-a-kind. The curtains are made using flannel receiving blankets. An extra one was used for cutting out tab tops. Glue or fusing tape replaces a sewing machine here (though you can always opt to use yours). The tiny finger-puppets attach to the tabs with hot glue, forming a colorful line-up of furry friends. This window's sure to be a source of endless delight for young eyes.

Supplies:

3 receiving blankets

5 to 10 small stuffed animals (these are finger puppets)

Fusing tape or fabric glue

Hot glue gun and glue sticks

Decorative pole rod

1. For tabs: Cut ten 5" x 11" strips from one of the receiving blankets. Fold each edge of strip so that they meet in the middle back and glue.

2. Fold the tabs in half and glue evenly spaced across the top of the two receiving blankets.

3. Hot glue the stuffed animals to the front of each tab.

4. Slip the tabs over the pole.

BUTTON, BUTTON

What can top a nursery window cleverly curtained with a receiving blanket? This ultra-easy idea makes ingenious use of coordinating baby washcloths and novelty buttons to form a fresh valance trim. Decorative buttons secure each cloth onto the pole, varying shades of green and blue to accent the lime check. This breezy look is a natural for baby's bathroom too.

Supplies:

Baby washcloths   2 receiving blankets

Decorative wooden buttons

Fusing tape or fabric glue

Needle and thread

2 spring-tension rods

1. Make a casing to fit the rod in the top of each blanket using fusing tape or fabric glue.

2. Fold each washcloth in half diagonally and sew a button to the front corner, through both layers of the washcloth.

3. Slip the washcloths over the spring rod, overlapping them slightly and attach the rod to the upper portion of window to form a valance.

4. Thread the two curtain panels on the other spring rod and attach to window, café style.

AWASH IN COLOR

Bright baby washcloths and dotted rings (actually linking toys) combine to create a wonderfully clever window in an infant's bathroom or nursery. The washline-style topper forms a multi-colored accent for the lime-checked curtain, made of a receiving blanket. The curtain is constructed using fusing tape and the valance is hooked up in seconds. This cute is this easy? Amazing, but true!

Supplies:

Baby washcloths

2 receiving blankets

8 hooks

Fusing tape or fabric glue

Curtain rod

Spring-tension rod

1. Make a casing to fit the rod in the top of each blanket using fusing tape or fabric glue.

2. Thread the curtain panels onto a spring rod. Attach the rod to the window, café style.

3. Clip the rings to the top of the wash cloths linking them together. If you can't find these particular rings, you can also use clip hooks.

4. Slip the rings onto the rod to hang as a valance.

DOTS IN BLOOM

Here's a wispy, feminine look for a girl's room or nursery. A halo of pretty dots and flower blossoms tops off a floral decorative scheme. The hems and casings for this sheer pouf are easily formed with glue or fusing tape, then the faux flowers slip into the casement along the bottom edge. The blooms lend weight, shape and soft color to the window treatment, enhancing the look of the whole room.

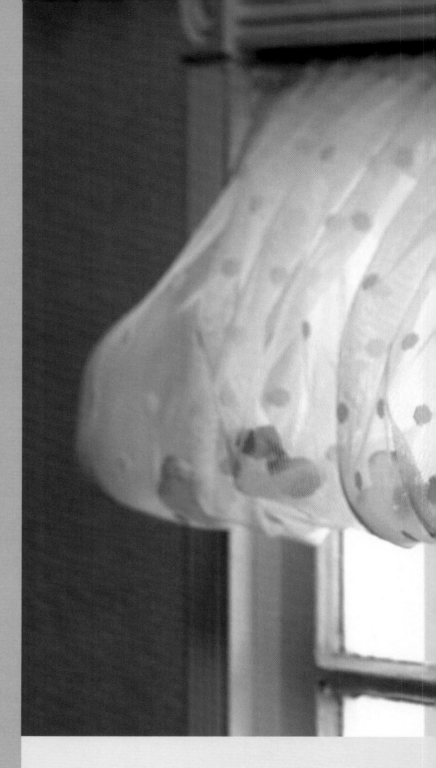

Supplies:
Sheer fabric with dot pattern
Small silk petals in various colors
2 spring-tension rods
Fabric glue or fusing tape

1. Measure the window.

2. Cut the fabric to that measurement adding enough for hems and casings.

3. Press the sides, top and bottom.

4. Hem sides using fusing tape or fabric glue.

5. Create casings at top and bottom of the panel using fusing tape or fabric glue.

6. Thread the casings on the rods. Mount one rod at top of window. Fold bottom of panel up and behind to meet top rod and mount just below it. This will create the pouf.

7. Sprinkle the silk petals inside the pouf.

Supplies:

Receiving blankets, 3 green-and-white check, 1 print (we used one with cars, planes and truck designs)

Fusing tape or fabric glue

Spring-tension rod

Conventional rod

1. For curtains: Make a casing to fit the rod in the top of each blanket using fusing tape or fabric glue.

2. Thread the curtain panels onto a spring rod. Attach the rod to the window, café style.

3. For ruffled valance: Cut the third green blanket in half. Make a hem at the bottom of each piece using fabric glue or fusing tape.

4. Turn down the top to form a casing with a 1" ruffle (see page 93).

5. Cut two pieces of the print blanket the same width as the green valance piece, but about 2½" shorter in length. Hem each piece.

6. Place the right side of the finished green piece on the wrong side of the print piece with about 4" of the printed piece extending above and about 2½" of the green piece extending below (A). Fold the top 4" piece down over the back (B).

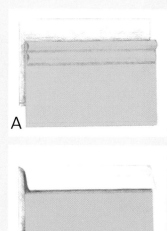

A

B

7. Glue or fuse the print piece to make the ruffle and casing following the fused lines of the green piece (C).

(Hint: On both pieces, be sure to glue the ruffle seams before gluing the bottom edge of the casing.)

C

BABY BLANKET VALANCE

With window treatments like this, you must be a whiz with a sewing machine, right? You can use a machine if you like, but this fetching nursery look was created entirely with fusing tape and receiving blankets. Amazing...when you look at the flouncy, layered valance and gathered curtains in this baby-boy perfect combination of patterns. You and your iron can create a look straight out of a trendy decorating magazine!

RIBBON-TAB CURTAINS

If your little girl loves to wear glossy hair ribbons, wait until she sees the tab tops on her beautiful new bedroom curtains! Color coordinated to match a harlequin pastel fabric, these tabs are made of shiny satin ribbons, each sporting an additional tie-on streamer to form a lovely flounce. The curtains are made with fusing tape or fabric glue, and glue also secures the tabs. Voila, you're a hero—now add to your status and paint the coordinating finials!

Supplies:

Pastel fabric (Laura Ashley)

Pink satin ribbon – ½" wide

Fusing tape or fabric glue

Decorative pole rod and finial (see page 81)

1. Cut two panels of fabric to fit the window allowing for hems on all four sides (see measuring instructions, page 92).

2. Press, then hem all four sides using fusing tape or fabric glue.

3. To make the ribbon tabs, cut ten lengths of ribbon 10". Fold each end of the ribbon under about ¼" for hem and glue. Fold the tabs in half and glue them evenly spaced across the top of the panels.

4. Cut ten more pieces of ribbon 18". Tie these pieces around each tab and let them hang loosely to the front of the panel.

5. Slip the tabs over the rod.

Idea

Sew buttons or silk flowers at the end of each tab as an alternative to the ribbon ties.

Or use an assortment of different colored ribbons for tabs to correspond with the colors in the fabric.

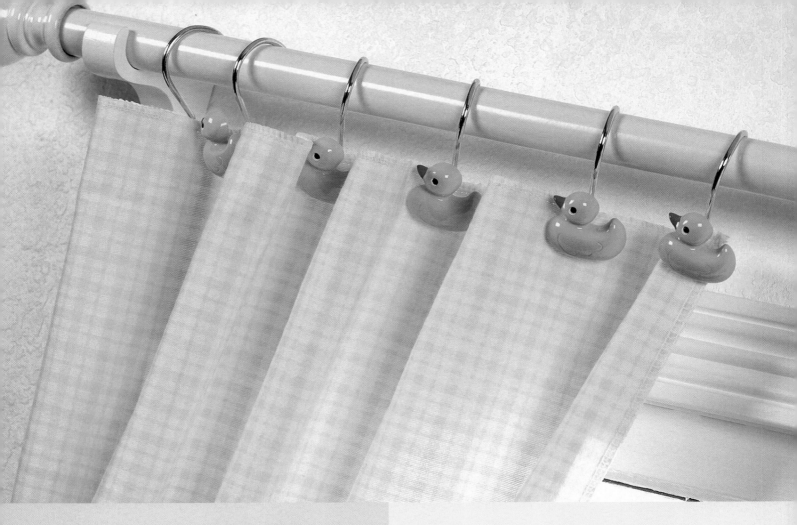

DUCKIE PARADE

Some shower curtain rings are so cute it would be a shame to confine them to the bathtub. This set features shiny yellow ducks and makes a sweet, splashy addition to a nursery or bathroom window. The rings hold up yellow plaid curtains made of receiving blankets. Allow thirty minutes of your busy day to create these curtains, and you're done! This is a "couldn't-be-easier" window treatment for a wee one's abode.

Supplies:

2 yellow-and-white plaid receiving blankets

Rubber duckie shower curtain hooks

Eyelets

Eyelet tool

Decorative pole rod

1. Using a craft knife, make small holes evenly spaced across the top of the receiving blankets (following manufacturer's instructions with eyelet kit).

2. Add eyelets using the eyelet tool.

3. Slip the shower curtain hooks into the eyelets.

4. Attach the hooks to the curtain rod.

TEA TOWEL TREATMENTS

LIME FIESTA

The lively striped trim on a set of green tea towels and napkins inspires a window treatment idea with south of the border flair. There's no need to fuss with the fabric; you simply glue strips of vivid bead trimming to towel ends and napkin corners. The towels are hung with ring clips, the napkins folded over the rod to form an easy valance. More bead trim cinches each curtain, finishing a vibrant look that's pure fun.

Supplies:

2 tea towels and napkins with ribbon trim

Beaded trim

Fabric glue

Clip-on rings and curtain rod

1. Glue the beaded trim along one short edge of each tea towel.

2. Cut off one strand of a bead and glue to one corner of each napkin.

3. Clip rings onto the two panels and slide over the rod.

4. Fold the two napkins diagonally and place them slightly overlapping over the rod.

5. Use the excess beaded trim to create tie backs.

Supplies:

2 tea towels with a tea pot border

Small cookie cutters

Other tea implements (strainers, teaspoons, etc.)

Green ribbon, ¼" wide

Clip-on rings

Curtain rod

1. Clip the rings to the top edge of the two towels.

2. Cut the ribbon in various lengths as desired. Thread ribbon through the cookie cutters and tea utensils, then arrange them across the tea towels to decide on placement.

3. Clip the two ends of the ribbon into the rings. Thread the rings onto the rod.

TEA SPOT

Teapot-trimmed tea towels make for a fresh window treatment, so apropos for a tea lover's kitchen nook. These curtains are literally clipped up in minutes, leaving plenty of time for a little creative expansion on the theme. The unique valance is made of teapot shaped cookie cutters, teaspoons, strainers and other tea-related paraphernalia. All are hung from the curtain clasps with green ribbon for a perfectly coordinated window ensemble.

KITCHEN LINENS

Tea towels and cloth napkins come in such pretty patterns, a favorite set can inspire a creative new look for your kitchen windows. These cheery, red-and-white curtains are made with linen towels embellished with cut-outs from coordinating fabric featuring redwork-like embroidery. Double-sided fusible web makes it easy to affix the fabric squares. The striped tabs are made using coordinating napkins. There's no end to the clever, linen-inspired designs you can come up with for your small windows.

Supplies:

2 red-and-white tea towels

Coordinating napkins

Redwork-themed fabric

Double-sided fusible web

Fusing tape or fabric glue

Decorative pole rod

1. Cut a piece of the redwork print fabric and following manufacturer's instructions, fuse the fabric to the web.

2. Cut out the squares, remove the backing paper and fuse squares to the tea towels (refer to photo for placement).

3. To make the tabs: Cut ten strips 2" x 7" from the coordinating napkins. The napkins are already hemmed, but you will need to hem the sides of the tabs. Fold the tab edges in about ¼" and glue.

4. Fold the tabs and glue them evenly spaced to top of panels (make sure hemmed side of tab is on the front of curtain).

5. Slide the panels over the rod.

Idea

Look for vintage tea towels, napkins and other linens when designing your window treatments. Search for ones with pretty embroidery or lace edges. Interesting pieces of damaged linens can be cut up and fused to fabric to decorate curtains

APPLES ALL DAY

This creative window treatment conjures up spiced cider and warm pie, and it's so easy, you'll want to make varying spring and summer versions as well. Red-and-white checked tea towels form the swag, but the real stars here are the hardware and accessories. A red-painted dowel, faux apple finials and a garland string of mini-apples pulls this great look together.

Supplies:

2 red-and-white checked napkins

Apple garland and 2 faux apples

1½" diameter dowel

Red acrylic paint and paintbrush

Hot glue gun and glue sticks

1. Paint the dowel red. Hot glue the apples to each end of rod for finials.

2. Fold the two napkins diagonally and place over the rod to create a valance.

3. Drape the apple garland over the valance. Glue ends of garland behind the apple finials to secure.

5

HANG-UPS

Supplies:

Assorted colors of glass or plastic beads

Assorted colors of drinking straws

Heavy-duty thread

Curtain rod and finial (see page 82)

1. Hang curtain rod.

2. Measure from the top of the rod to where you want the curtain to end. Cut a length of thread to this measurement adding 8".

3. Tie a bead to one end of the thread.

4. Lay the thread on a table and lay out the straws and beads next to it to plan your pattern.

5. Thread on the beads and the straws leaving about 8" at the end. Thread only beads onto the last 8". Tie this into a loop and make a knot.

6. Slide the loops on the rod. If desired, hang the beaded curtains over a sheer panel (as pictured).

BEAD SURPRISE

Here's a twist on beaded curtains and a creative project that a girl or teen will enjoy. She'll amaze her friends with this pretty bedroom-window brightener, combining shiny beads with matching, colored drinking straws. Each strand starts with a beaded bracelet-style hanger, then is interspersed with straws and more beads. Hung to front a sheer curtain, this fringe will play in the sunlight to set the beads to sparkling and the straws aglow!

Supplies:

Assorted lengths of ribbon (we used red, yellow, green and purple)

Silk flowers

Hot glue gun and glue sticks

Spring-tension rod

1. Cut ribbon to fit the window opening, adding enough to go around the rod. You can use ribbon of the same or different widths.

2. Choose silk flowers that coordinate with the ribbon colors. Cut leaves off of the flowers. Then cut the back of flowers so that they lay flat. Glue the flowers at varying lengths to the ribbon.

3. Turn the ribbon over at the top to create a loop and glue. Thread the ribbons onto the rod.

4. Trim any of the ribbon lengths as necessary to fit the window.

BLOOMING COLOR

When ordinary just won't do for a girl or teen's window accent, create a curtain of bright ribbon streamers to cascade from above. Strewn with an eclectic variety of glue-on silk flowers, this window lets a girl "go floral" in a unique, clever way. A variety of themes can be created with lightweight objects and ribbon strips, which are looped over a rod and glued for easy mount. This idea can stand alone or accessorize curtains.

Supplies:

Skeleton leaves (silver, gold, bronze, lavender)

Wire edged ribbon, bronze, ⅛" wide

Craft glue

Spring-tension rod

1. Cut ribbon in various lengths.

2. Glue a skeleton leaf to the end of each length.

3. Tie the other end of the ribbon around the curtain rod.

4. Hang the ribbons in front of a sheer panel if desired.

Hint

Skeleton leaves are available in many sizes and colors at your local craft or specialty paper store. If you can only find the natural versions, you can easily paint them using acrylic paint. Add a small amount of water to the paint to create a wash to use for painting the leaves.

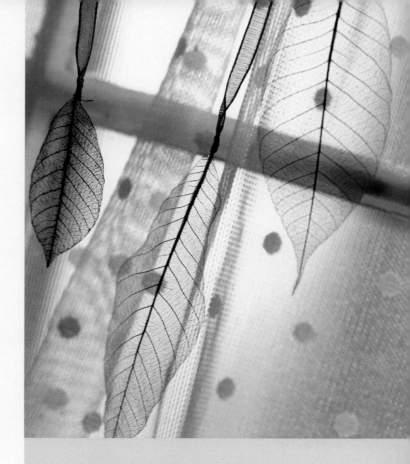

SHEER BEAUTY

There's something about filmy, sheer material that imparts a languid, ethereal feeling, and where one piece is lovely, a layered look can be stunning. This window tops gauzy, dot-pattern fabric with strands of sheer ribbon, each dangling a delicate, see-through skeleton leaf. The sunlight reveals a pleasing mix of outlined shapes and whispery color in shades of bronze, gold and lavender. In fading light, this window "paints" a serene picture of falling leaves and snowflakes!

Supplies:

Shells and starfish

Silver spray paint

Gold metallic paint

Small scruffy brush

Wire edge ribbon,
silver, $\frac{1}{8}$" wide

Small drill

1. Drill a hole in the top of each shell.

2. Spray paint the shells silver. Let dry.

3. With a scruffy (old) brush, paint gold areas here and there on the shells (refer to photo).

4. Cut ribbon in various lengths. Thread the ribbon through the holes in the shells and tie the other end around the rod.

5. If desired, hang a sheer panel in the window behind the hanging shells.

SEASHELL CASCADE

Hung from a curtain rod, strings of shells turn a plain curtain into one that makes a distinct decorative statement. This look would be wonderful for a beach cottage or perhaps for the bedroom of a young one with seagoing dreams. Each shell is painted metallic silver with gold accents, and then hung from silvery ribbon strands of differing lengths. This window mobile works well with sheer curtains or could also stand alone.

6

HOOK-UPS

Supplies:

Polka dot fabric

Bright colored hair bands

Fabric glue

Needle and thread

Spring-tension rod

1. Cut two panels of polka dot fabric to fit the window allowing for hems on all four sides.

2. Press, then hem all four sides using fusing tape or fabric glue.

PONYTAIL POLKA

A bright, multi-colored rainbow of hair bands is put to innovative use for this jazzy curtain set, perfect for a baby or child's room. Chosen in colors to match the bold print of the fabric, these soft circles are ideal, whimsical curtain rings to accessorize a young one's windows. The hair bands can be glued on to the curtains or you can tack them with a needle and thread. So clever!

3. Using fabric glue, affix the hair bands evenly spaced along the top of the two panels. Secure the bands by tacking with a needle and thread, if desired.

4. Slip the colorful rings over the rod.

BLUE WILLOW CURTAINS

This creative window treatment celebrates the beauty of a favorite china pattern, and lets you show off a plate and cup display along with your curtains. A white plate rack does double duty here, displaying pretty dishes while holding up a matching tab-top curtain panel. Each panel pocket also displays a paper napkin in a coordinating blue and white pattern—an extra touch that really pulls this innovative look together.

Supplies:

White plate rack

Tab top pocket panel, white

4 blue willow cups and saucers (any pattern will do)

Blue and white paper napkins (to match plate design)

1. Hang the plate rack above the window.

2. Cut the paper napkins into rectangles to fit pockets and insert them randomly as desired.

3. Hang the panel onto the hooks of the plate rack.

4. Place cups and saucers in the rack.

Idea

Try placing small pieces of your kitchen or dining room wallpaper in the curtain pockets to coordinate with the room.

Use teacups and saucers received as gifts or handed down through the family for a real conversation piece.

COAT RACK CURTAINS

Decorative peg racks are most often used to hang coats or hats, but they also make perfect curtain hangers. These decorative pieces can be found in carved wood and other interesting materials and can be left natural or painted to suit. Two racks placed above a window hang permanent accent curtains with flair. This fringed scarf is tied onto the pegs with pieces of fringe for a drapery, casual look.

Supplies:
Decorative coat or hat rack
Scarves with fringe

1. Hang the racks on either side of a wide window or just one over a narrow window.

2. Tie the fringe loosely on the pegs to drape slightly.

INDONESIAN TEXTILE DISPLAY

Import stores carry unique decorative items from the far corners, and many can be creatively adapted for window treatments. Used in Indonesia to display fabric, these lovely, carved-wood "textile hangers" make a wonderful set of curtain rods. Attached side by side above the window, they hold curtains made of Indian scarves. The fold-over fringe forms a pretty valance, finishing an exotic window solution that's unbelievably easy.

Supplies:

2 textile hangers (or just one for a narrow window)

2 scarves with fringed ends

1. Hang the textile hangers above the window.

2. Thread the scarves through the slot, hanging slightly down on the front to form valances.

COLOR SPIN

Accessorized with shiny pinwheels, these bright, rainbow-striped curtains help set a playful mood in a child's primary-colored bedroom or playroom. After all, a creative atmosphere helps keep a young mind awhirl with bright ideas! Hemmed with fusing tape, the fabric attaches easily to a spring rod with clip-on rings. Color-coordinated pinwheels, glued to each hook, add a child-pleasing spin to this fun window treatment.

Supplies:

Striped and solid fabric

Pinwheels on sticks (these were a set of swizzle sticks from an import store)

Fusing tape or fabric glue

Hot glue gun and glue sticks

Clip hooks

Spring-tension rod and conventional rod

1. Cut enough fabric to make two panels of the striped fabric and a valance of the solid.

2. Glue or fuse hems on all four sides of the two panels.

3. Glue or fuse the hems of the valance. Create a casing in the valance big enough to fit the rod you're using. Slip the valance on the conventional rod.

4. Clip the hooks evenly spaced across the top of the two panels.

5. Remove the pinwheels from the sticks and hot glue them to the front of the clips.

6. Slip the panels onto the spring-tension rod.

SKIPPER'S WINDOW

For a room with a nautical theme, this clever window accent is ship-shape! What's more, it's made with inexpensive pieces, and putting it together is a breeze. The project starts with an oar-shaped peg-board painted blue and embellished with a miniature boat. Then, fish netting is hung from the pegs, standing ready to catch an assortment of star fish. (Lucky you—the only fishing you have to do is at your local craft store.)

Supplies:

Wooden oar with pegs (from craft store or craft department of a fabric store)

Fish net

Star fish, assorted sizes

Toy sailboat

Blue and white acrylic paint

Paintbrush

Sandpaper

Glue gun

1. Paint the oar white. Let dry and add a coat of the blue paint. Let dry.

2. Sand the oar to give it an aged appearance.

3. Hot glue the toy sailboat to the wide part of the oar.

4. Hang the oar above the window.

5. Hang the fish net on the pegs.

6. Attach the star fish either by gluing or wiring onto the net.

7. Trim the net to fit the window. Use a bit of twine or rope as a tieback, if desired.

BEADED RINGS

With its ivory color and loose textured weave, this gorgeous fabric imparts a natural look. How best to flatter it? Wooden curtain rings are an obvious choice. Each curtain ring boasts a dangling strand of wooden and gold-tone beads. These pretty accents clip into place, along with the no-sew panels, for an "expensive" designer look without the designer price.

Supplies:

Ivory fabric with woven design

Fusing tape or fabric glue

Wooden and gold beads and wire

Wooden clip hooks and decorative pole rod

1. Fuse or glue hems on all four sides.

2. String the beads on wire (about 5 to a strand). Leave one end of the wire extended about 2". Form a small loop on the other end of the wire using a needlenose pliers.

3. Clip the hooks onto the top edge of the panel and the ends of the wire into the hooks.

4. Slip the hooks over the rod.

7

AND MORE

Anyone who's ever needed emergency window coverings is familiar with handy, inexpensive paper shades. A little creative embellishment can transform these temporary shades into something you won't mind keeping around longer.

Just look at the projects at left—fabric covered shades complete the décor of this room, coordinating nicely with the pillows and lampshade. And anyone who's had to think of ways to cover an arched window, need look no more. These shades can hang in a traditional window or be fan-folded to fit an arched one.

Paper shades can be decorated by covering with fabric, handmade paper, giftwrap, and wallpaper. They can be painted, stamped, sponged and stenciled. So let your imagination go wild and create a special window treatment that's either temporary or here to stay. These shades are fun, easy and inexpensive

The shade above was covered with an interesting Asian paper featuring large, graphic Chinese characters. The clips (which are included in the Redi-shade package) have been decorated with origami cranes. Simply hot glue any decoration such as silk flowers, painted wooden cutouts, tassels or ribbons to the clips to achieve just the right look for your own creation.

PRETTY PAPER

Covered with a layer of fancy handmade paper, this shade now boasts new texture and beauty. The paper smooths on in minutes with the help of spray glue, then the shade's own adhesive strip attaches to the top of the window. There are so many beautiful handmade papers available. You can choose from a natural looking paper as the one pictured here or select a paper embedded with rose petals, colorful mulberry papers, or even metallics. The sky's the limit.

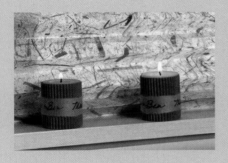

Supplies:

1 paper shade (Redi-Shade)

Large sheet of handmade paper

Spray adhesive

Ruler

Craft knife and scissors

1. Measure the length and width of the window (inside the casing). Don't cut the shade to size until after applying paper.

2. Using scissors, cut the decorative paper to the desired width and length. Be sure to add an extra inch or two to the width as the paper may angle during application. The excess paper can be trimmed off later.

3. Cover work surface with a drop cloth.

Lay the shade on surface with top edge of tape strip nearest you.

4. Flatten out the shade as much as possible. Using the spray adhesive, spray the first two or three pleats and carefully press the paper into the glue.

5. Spraying six to eight pleats at a time, continue to press the paper onto the shade, keeping it as straight as possible.

6. Once all the paper is applied, re-pleat by simply folding along the original pleat lines.

7. Using a craft knife or scissors, trim the side edges of the shade to the desired width. Trim the shade to the desired length, using scissors.

8. Hang using the adhesive strip, which comes on the shade, to the top of the window.

Supplies:

Table runner with tassels

Fusing tape or fabric glue

Sheer panel

Decorative pole rod

Spring-tension rod

1. Cut the table runner in half.

2. Turn the raw edges over to form casings (measure the rod you'll be using to determine the casing size). Press, then glue to form the casing.

3. Slip the runners over the decorative pole.

4. We hung the runners on either side of a sheer panel which is hung on a spring-tension rod.

☀ Idea

Use decorative placemats draped over a rod for a quick and easy valance treatment.

Lace table runners can also be sewn or draped for a different treatment.

A lace tablecloth could be used as a swag for the window.

Adding tassels to purchased curtains and drapes creates a touch of elegance. Tassels can be purchased at fabric, craft and home decor stores.

NO-HASSLE TASSELS

Before you pass up that pretty table runner on sale at the decorator shop, stop to consider its potential as a unique window accent! Embellished with a gold tassel on each end, this rich, floral print runner can become a lovely window feature for the dining room. The runner is simply cut in half, the pieces hung on a rod to form a unique swag. Fusing tape or glue quickly creates the necessary casings, and then...you're done!

Supplies:

Purchased bamboo curtain

Leaf: gold, silver and variegated

Spray-on leaf adhesive

Soft cloth

1. Tape protective paper or drop cloth to a wall where you'll be painting the curtain to completely cover the area. Hang up the curtain.

2. Working in small areas at a time and starting at the top of the curtain, spray with adhesive. Allow to dry for about 30 minutes until just tacky.

3. Apply the sheets of leaf in random spots across the bamboo—varying the shades of gold, silver and variegated.

4. With a soft cloth, rub the bamboo strands to wipe away excess leaf.

5. Continue these steps all the way down the curtain.

GOLDEN BAMBOO

Inexpensive bamboo curtains lend an exotic feel and blend well with natural and ethnic style furnishings. This example has been embellished with metallic leafing, elevating its decorative status into the realm of artistic conversation piece. Gold, silver and variegated leafing is applied randomly across adhesive-sprayed bamboo strands, then hand rubbed with a soft cloth. This unique curtain (or room divider) will glow and shimmer in the sunlight!

8

TIEBACKS

TIEBACKS

Just as accessories change the look of a simple outfit, new curtain tiebacks can transform your window treatments. From casual to elegant, traditional to modern, tiebacks help set a mood and can completely change the look of your curtains. These next pages illustrate this concept, showing a variety of treatments. While many types of ready-made tiebacks are available for purchase, all of these shown have been quickly put together with inexpensive craft store finds or items you might have at home. Remember, always keep your eye out for interesting objects at swap meets or antique stores. You never know when you'll find your next tieback idea!

BEADED FRUIT

1. Attach a cup hook to the desired position near the window casing.

2. Wrap the wire of the fruit around each panel and twist to secure.

3. Attach the excess wire to the cup hook.

CHINESE KNOTTED

FOLK ART

1. Attach a cup hook to the desired position near window casing.

2. Attach the Chinese decoration to a length of red cord using wire. Wrap the cord around the curtain.

3. Tie the cord to the cup hooks.

1. Wrap two colorful Mexican scarves around the panels and tie in a square knot.

2. Attach the tin bird to scarves using self adhesive hook and loop dots.

3. Attach tiebacks using push pins.

ANTIQUE BROACH

1. Attach a broach to a length of elegant ribbon.

2. Wrap ribbon around curtain. Use a small nail or pushpin hidden under the back of the ribbon to attach to the wall.

FLORAL & RIBBON

1. Add a pretty ribbon bow to the back of a wired bouquet of silk flowers.

2. Wrap the wires of the bouquet around the panel.

3. Attach the wire to a cup hook.

GOLDEN ROSETTE

1. Cut a 2" circle of cardboard. Coil gold cord into a circle and glue to cardboard. Glue a tassel to the front.

2. Cut ribbon into six 4" pieces. Fold and glue ribbon to the back of the coiled cord forming a rosette.

3. Braid three strands of cord and knot on each end. Glue the rosette to the length of cord and tie around the curtain. Attach cord to cup hook.

ANIMAL PRINT

1. Wrap ribbon around the curtains and glue in the back to secure, overlapping ends about 2".

2. Insert pushpin through overlapped area into wall behind curtains.

HEADBAND HELPER

Stretchy headbands make wonderful tie-backs for these unbelievably easy accent curtains, made from pre-hemmed receiving blankets. The pretty fabric is cinched with a coordinating bow-topped headband, creating a perfectly delightful window dressing for a little girl's bedroom or bathroom. Handy fusing tape forms a rod casing for the curtain for easy hanging, then just slip on the headband!

Supplies:

2 receiving blankets

2 stretchy headbands

Fusing tape or fabric glue

Spring-tension rod

Pushpins

1. Make a casing in the top of each blanket using fusing tape or fabric glue.

2. Thread the curtain panels onto a spring rod.

3. Slip the headbands around the curtains and attach in back using pushpins.

BATHTIME DUCKS

If baby's bathroom needs window dressing, you can't go wrong with this darling "rubber duckie" theme. Little stuffed ducklings help hold back pink-dotted curtains made of pretty receiving blankets. Jumbo chenille rickrack strips twist together to help unify the pink and yellow color scheme. This is so cute you might want to incorporate the theme into the nursery as well!

Supplies:

2 pink receiving blankets

Stuffed animal

Pink and yellow chenille rickrack

Fusing tape or fabric glue

Spring-tension rod

1. Make a casing in the top of each blanket using fusing tape or fabric glue.

2. Braid the pink and yellow rickrack together and glue the ends to secure. Use the rickrack to tie back each panel. Hot glue the stuffed animal to front of the tiebacks.

3. Use a cup hook to attach the tieback.

ALL BUTTONED UP

Here's a creative way to make use of stray buttons or some pretty ones you might find at a flea market or garage sale. These metallic tie-backs add shine and character to a curtained window treatment, while your own selected buttons will make a one-of-a-kind home accent. Simply string your assortment onto metallic cord, then wrap the tiebacks around the panels and secure onto hooks or nails.

Supplies:

Assortment of gold buttons

Metallic cord

Needle

Cup hooks

1. String the buttons randomly onto the cord using a needle. Knot the ends.

2. Wrap the button strand around curtains and attach ends of cord to cup hooks.

9

FINIALS

VERDIGRIS ON A BUDGET

This rod and finial set would easily pass for stylish, metallic window hardware found in upscale stores, but this model is much less pricey. Faux finish spray-on paint helps create a gorgeous, gleaming verdigris surface on a wooden dowel and wooden pieces purchased at a craft store. It looks so real no one would suspect, and the money you save can go toward your curtain fabric!

(Instructions on page 84)

GOLDEN GLOW

Metallic fabrics, so popular now for window treatments, are set off beautifully with gleaming metallic rods and finials. This antique-gold curtain hardware is elegant, and only looks expensive because it's made of metallic-painted wood pieces. Home improvement and craft store purchases create this look, but who would know? This luxury treatment would add a touch of class to any living, dining or bedroom.

(Instructions on page 84)

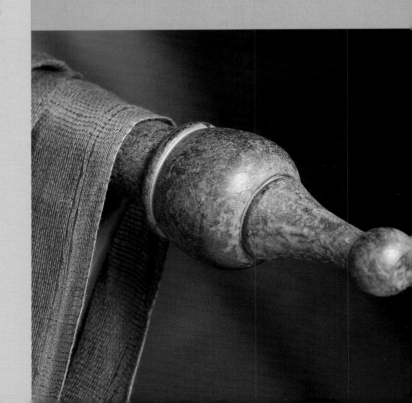

FAIRYTALE FINIALS

You've found the perfect colorful curtain fabric for your baby or child's room, now extend the fun further and paint wooden finials to match! At a craft store, select a few interesting wood pieces to glue together; these are made with a wooden peg atop an upside down candleholder. Then, have great fun mixing and matching colors from your fabric to create an eclectic, patterned design. These custom pieces give your windows a spectacular finish, at a fraction of the cost!

(Instructions on page 84)

WINDOW ART

When the curtains are extraordinary, how can the window hardware be anything but? No need to hunt for a perfect set-up in stores—you can paint your own dowel and finials for a true custom look. Wooden pieces from the craft store and paint colors that are "just-so" help you create coordinating hardware that can elevate your windows to the status of art. The fun you have doing it is just an added bonus!

(Instructions on page 84)

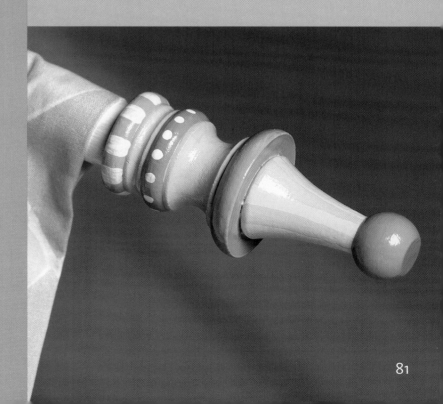

ISLAND GLASS

Hardware is important to the total look of the window, so be sure to show off custom curtains with beautiful, one-of-a-kind finials. Think "finials" whenever you prowl through unique gift and import shops, because the decorative possibilities are endless. Here, a pair of glass floats, embellished with crisscrossing raffia, help turn a bamboo pole into an exotic mount for island-style curtains.

(Instructions on page 85)

BEAD SURPRISE

It's only fitting that multi-colored, bead curtains are set off with a brightly painted bead finial. A large, wooden bead and wooden ring are painted in two colors to coordinate with this unique girl's bedroom window treatment. The ring resembles a bangle bracelet just as the curtain "rings" look like beaded bracelets. It slips over the painted dowel just before the wood bead is glued to the end.

(Instructions on page 85)

TOTALLY TOILE

Toile's storybook patterns are timeless and beautiful, and many devotees love them. True fans enjoy combining toile patterns together, matching colors to make a unique decorative statement. This curtained window with coordinated finial lets a toile-lover indulge to her heart's content. Actually made of wood, the finials are covered, decoupage-style, with a toile pattern napkin. Paper or fabric works equally as well, smoothing on easily with decoupage medium and your fingertips.

(Instructions on page 85)

AFFORDABLE MARBLE

Shiny marble is always eye-catching, and adds decorative weight and drama wherever it's placed. This window treatment is one example, though this beautiful finial only looks like marble! This showy piece is actually made of wood, coated with layers of glass paint to achieve a glossy, multi-faceted look. A basecoat of white acrylic paint is followed by drizzles of colorful glass paint that drip to create unique, marble-esque patterns.

(Instructions on page 85)

GOLDEN GLOW (pg. 80)

Supplies:

1½" round dowel
2 unpainted wooden finials
Antique Gold spray paint kit
 (American Accents)
Varnish or sealer

1. Have the dowel cut to fit your window.

2. Use the spray painting kit to paint the dowel and the finials following the manufacturer's instructions. Allow to dry. Brush on sealer or varnish.

3. Screw the finials to the dowel.

VERDIGRIS ON A BUDGET (pg. 80)

Supplies:

1" round dowel
Patina spray paint kit
 (American Accents)
2 wooden pegs and 2 wood
 candle cups(from craft store)
Wood glue
Varnish or sealer

1. Have the dowel cut to fit your window.

2. Glue the wooden peg to the bottom of the candle cup with wood glue to make the finial.

3. Using the patina kit, follow the manufacturer's directions for painting the dowel and finials. Let dry. Brush on sealer or varnish.

4. Glue the finials to each end of the dowel.

WINDOW ART (pg. 81)

Supplies:

2 1½" wooden ball knobs
2 2" wooden candleholders
Acrylic paints (to coordinate
 with your fabric)
Foam brush
Small paintbrush
1" round dowel
Varnish or sealer
Wood glue

1. Have the dowel cut to fit your window.

2. Glue the wooden bead to the bottom of the candleholder.

3. Base the dowel and the wooden pieces with your main color (we used peach) using the foam brush.

4. Following the shapes of the wood pieces, paint with various colors. Add dots and stripes as desired (refer to photo on page 81 for suggested design). Let all pieces dry. Brush on sealer or varnish.

5. Fit the opening of the candleholder to the dowel and glue in place.

FAIRYTALE FINIALS (pg. 81)

Supplies:

1" round dowel
2 wooden pegs and 2 wooden
 candleholders (from craft store)
Various shades of acrylic paint
 (to match your fabric)
Small paintbrush
Foam brush
Wood glue
Varnish or sealer

1. Have the dowel cut to fit your window.

2. Glue the wooden peg to the bottom of the candleholder.

3. Base the dowel and the wooden pieces with your main color (we used pink) using acrylic paint and the foam brush.

4. Following the shapes of the wood pieces, paint with various colors. Add dots and stripes as desired. (refer to photo on page 81 for suggested design). Let all pieces dry. Brush on sealer or varnish.

5. Fit the opening of the candleholder to the dowel.

MAKING FINIALS

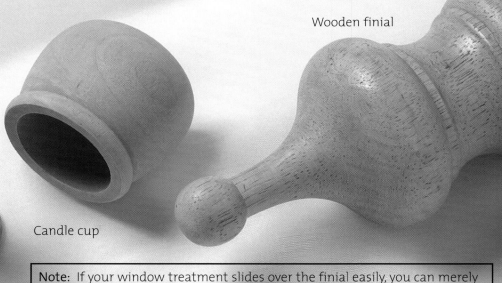

Wooden finial

Candle cup

Wooden ball knob

Wooden peg

Note: If your window treatment slides over the finial easily, you can merely glue the finial to the end of the dowel. If not, you'll need to add a dowel screw to the finial which you screw into your pre-drilled hole in the dowel.

BEAD SURPRISE (pg.82)

Supplies:

Dowel
2 wooden wheels
2 2½" wooden ball knobs
Acrylic paint, fuchsia and peach
Wood glue
Foam brush & small paintbrush
Varnish or sealer

1. Glue the wooden beads to the wooden wheels to make the finial.

2. Paint the dowel and bead fuchsia using the foam brush. With the small brush, paint the wheel peach.

3. Brush on varnish or sealer.

4. Glue the finials to each end of the dowel using wood glue.

ISLAND GLASS (pg. 82)

Supplies:

Bamboo pole (from garden supply department)
2 glass floats wrapped in raffia (Loose Ends)
Glue gun and glue sticks
Narrow rope or twine

1. Hot glue the glass floats to each end of the bamboo pole.

2. Glue the twine or rope around the pole where it meets the glass floats.

AFFORDABLE MARBLE (pg. 83)

Supplies:

1½" round dowel
Unpainted wooden finial
White acrylic paint
Assorted colors of transparent glass paint (Air Dry PermEnamel by Delta)
Foam brush
Wood glue

1. Paint the rod and finial with a basecoat of white acrylic paint using a foam brush. Allow to dry.

2. Set the finials on a small jar or glass to prop up. Drizzle coordinating colors of the glass paint onto the top of the finials and allow paint to drip down the sides creating a marbleized effect. Allow to dry.

3. Paint the rod a color to match the finials using acrylic paint and a foam brush.

4. Attach the finials to the rod using wood glue.

TOTALLY TOILE (pg.83)

Supplies:

1½" round dowel
2 unpainted wooden finials
Paper napkins, blue toile pattern
Mod Podge®

Foam brush
Varnish or sealer

1. Have the dowel cut to fit your window.

2. Basecoat the dowel and the finials white using a foam brush. Allow to dry.

3. Apply Mod Podge® on the back of the napkin using a foam brush and lay the napkin over the finial. Paint again with Mod Podge®. While it's still wet, smooth the napkin over the finial using your fingertips. Smooth out any wrinkles. Brush on more Mod Podge®, if the napkin gets dry, and keep smoothing. Smooth napkin to the underneath part of the finial and trim any excess paper to neaten.

4. Place the finials over the rod.

Wooden napkin ring

Wooden egg cup

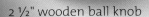

2 ½" wooden ball knob

Wooden egg

Wooden wheels

HOOKS

Think about the total look of the window treatment you want to create and choose hardware that enhances that look, rather than competes with it.

When you're considering ease of hanging, use hooks and clips. Nothing can be easier than just clipping these to the tops of your panel and slipping them onto a rod. There are so many types on the market to choose from. And don't forget to look for alternative types of hooks, too, such as shower curtain hooks, stationery clips, pushpins, even hair bands! (see page 52).

Examples of some hooks that can be used to create easy treatments:

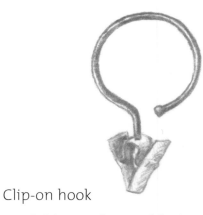

Clip-on hook

Available in white or black and metallic finishes.

Large clip-on hook with wooden ring

Wooden or plastic rings with clip-on hooks

Clip-on café ring, usually brass

HOOKS

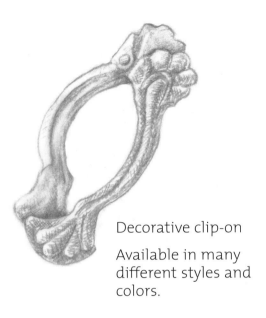

Decorative clip-on

Available in many different styles and colors.

Shower curtain rod hook

These are available in a multitude of designs and types. They're in the shower curtain department of home improvement and discount chain stores.

Alternative hooks

Binder clips - stationery store find

These are available in several sizes. Can be clipped on to the curtain and then hung using a tension wire (very European!).

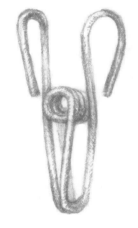

Plastic coated clips

Just clip onto curtain and hang on nails, decorated pushpins or thumbtacks.

There are rods and poles for nearly every curtain treatment. They come in a myriad of types and finishes. Some are available in sets with the rod, brackets and finials all in one package. There are rods and poles for inside and outside mounts, tension rods for lightweight treatments and U-shaped rods for rod-pocket curtains.

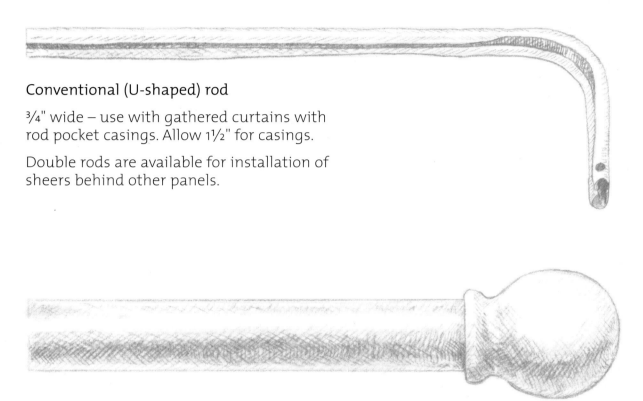

Conventional (U-shaped) rod

¾" wide – use with gathered curtains with rod pocket casings. Allow 1½" for casings.

Double rods are available for installation of sheers behind other panels.

Decorative pole rod

Can be used with gathered curtains or curtains on rings. The ends unscrew for easy curtain hanging. Available in several different finishes and designs.

Decorative metal rod

These are available in many different metallic finishes and styles. The ends screw off for easy curtain hanging.

RODS & POLES

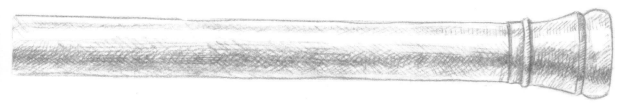

Shower curtain rod

When you don't want to pound nails into the wall or you need a temporary treatment, a shower rod could be just the answer. Mount inside windows.

Spring-tension rod

For inside window mounts. This is the most handy of all curtain rods. No tools are needed and they're extremely quick and easy to install.

Café curtain rod

You will need to hang brackets to hold this type of rod which mounts on the outside of the window.

ROD HOLDERS

Rod holders are available in several design types. They come in several finishes, many different materials and several designs. You can select brackets, sconces or decorative rod holders.

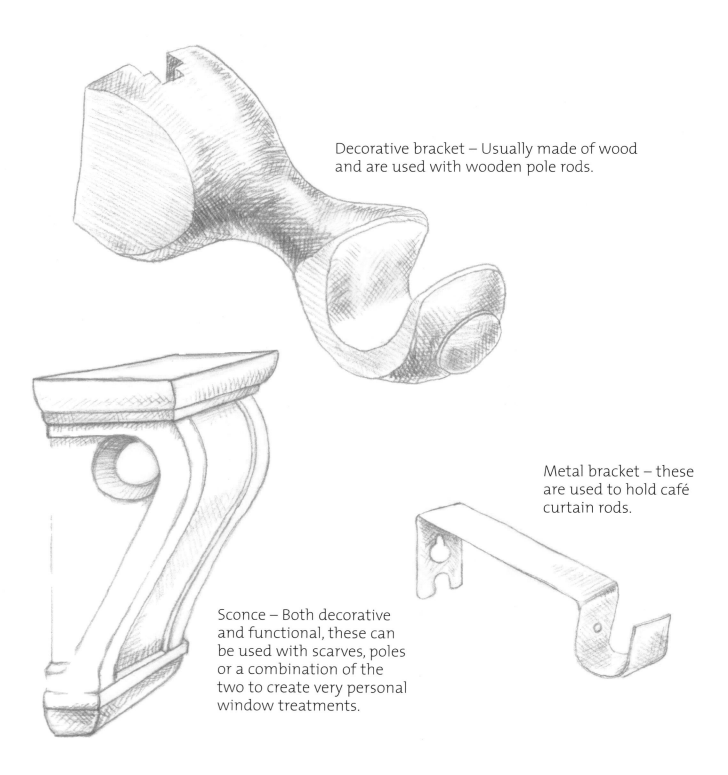

Decorative bracket – Usually made of wood and are used with wooden pole rods.

Metal bracket – these are used to hold café curtain rods.

Sconce – Both decorative and functional, these can be used with scarves, poles or a combination of the two to create very personal window treatments.

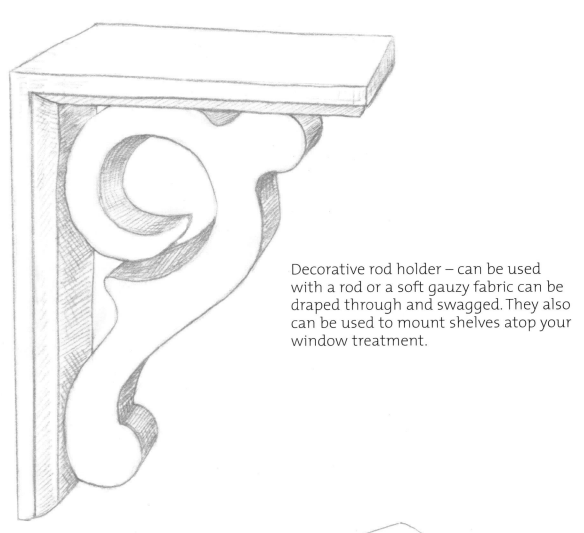

Decorative rod holder – can be used with a rod or a soft gauzy fabric can be draped through and swagged. They also can be used to mount shelves atop your window treatment.

Bracket – these are also for holding wooden poles. They're a bit smaller than the decorative bracket.
This one holds a 1" diameter pole.

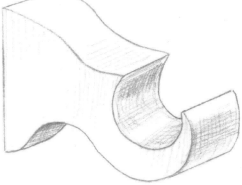

GENERAL INSTRUCTIONS

With fusible products and fabric glues available now, it's possible to create casual and elegant window treatments without sewing a stitch.

Everything in this book was made using paper backed fusible web, web tape, fusible notions, and fabric glue.

Estimating Supplies

We have not listed specific yardage amounts for any of the projects in this book because all windows are different. Read through all the instructions for your project, then take all measurements.

Measuring will be the most important step for successful results. See Calculating Fabric chart (page 94).

Any leftover scraps can be used to make coordinating projects (lampshades, pillows, placemats, and tiebacks).

If you need to match a print fabric, you'll need extra fabric. Measure design repeat. Multiply by the number of panels needed. If the design repeat is 18" and you need 3 panels, multiply 18" x 3. You'll need 54" (or 1½ yds) of extra fabric.

Measuring

Always use a metal measuring tape to get a precise measurement.

Measure each window individually because each one could have slightly different measurements.

Refer to the window diagram (page 94) to measure for different types of installation (inside or outside) and lengths (sill, apron, floor). Mount rods before measuring for length of treatment.

Selecting fabrics

We've used several types of fabric for the projects in this book, from light to medium weight cotton, decorator fabrics and sheers. All of them lent themselves to no-sew treatments.

Do not pre-wash fabrics before using them, washing will remove protective finishes which repel soiling.

Cutting fabric

Plan your cutting prior to starting the project. Press the fabric before cutting. Use a T-square or carpenter's square to make sure one end of the fabric is square.

After fabric has been squared, measure and mark cutting lines using a disappearing ink fabric pen or marking pencil. Cut fabric using a rotary cutter or sharp scissors.

Fusing

Follow the manufacturer's instructions for any fusible product you use. Always test the fusible products on a piece of scrap fabric prior to making your project.

Fusible products are available in different weights to use with most weights of fabric. Make sure you select the correct one for your fabric weight.

Gluing

We've used both fusing and gluing techniques for the projects in this book. We preferred using fabric glue because it's both easier and quicker to use than fusing tapes.

Making a Hem

Before hemming a selvage edge, clip it at 2" to 3" intervals and press to reduce any puckering.

Iron in all hems and casings prior to fusing or gluing to insure proper measurements.

Select a web tape width that is compatible with the hem you're planning. Fuse the tape along the edge on the wrong side of fabric. Remove paper backing. Fold along hemline to wrong side of fabric and fuse tape in place.

Making a casing

With wrong side of fabric facing up, fold top edge down the number of inches calculated for the casing add ¼" to ½" depending on the width of the fusing tape. Use fabric glue to seam in place. Use fusing tape along inside bottom edge of casing to seam in place.

Making a casing with a ruffle

Have wrong side of fabric facing up. Fold top edge down the number of inches calculated for the casing and ruffle. For example, for a 1" ruffle and 2" casing, you'll need to fold down 3¼" to 3½" (depending on the width of the fusing tape).

Press along top edge of fabric. Open fabric back up and measure down and mark for ruffle from fold line (example: 1" from fold line). Use fabric glue or fusing tape along marked line. Fold fabric back down and fuse or glue in place. Next use glue or fusing tape along inside of bottom edge to seam in place.

CALCULATING YARDAGE

(For no-sew curtains)

1. Measure window

2. Record measurements for your desired type of curtain or drape and where you will mount the rod.

3. Do the figuring:

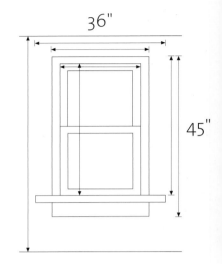

WIDTH		Example	Your Figures
Window Width _____		36"	_____
Desired fullness _____ 1½", 2" or 2½"	X	1.5	X _____
	=	54"	= _____
Width that fabric comes _____ (decorator fabric – 54" cotton type – 45")	÷	45"	÷ _____
Number of widths or panels __	=	1.9	= _____
Number of widths or panels __ (rounded)	=	2 (A)	= _____ (A)

LENGTH

		Example	Your Figures
Desired length _____		45"	_____
Hem (1" – 3") _____	+	1"	+ _____
Casing (to fit rod width + ½") __	+	2.5"	+ _____
Ruffle (if desired 1" – 3") _____	+	1"	+ _____
Total length _____	=	49.5" (B)	= _____ (B)
Number of widths or panels __	x	2 (A)	X _____ (A)
	=	99"	= _____
Number of inches in yd. _____	÷	36"	÷ _36"_
YARDAGE NEEDED _____	=	2.75	= _____

MEASUREMENTS

Copy this page, add your window measurements and take it with you when shopping for fabric.

Room _____

Room _____

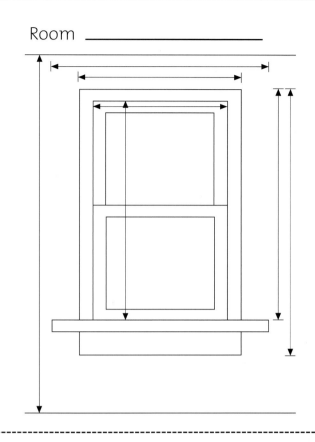

Room _____

Room _____

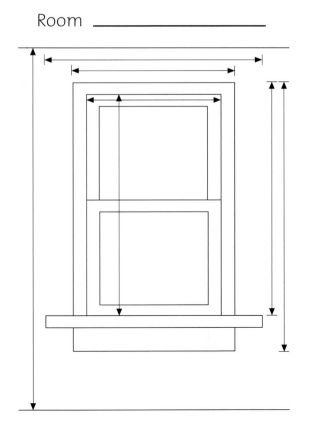

GLOSSARY

FUSING

Fuse – to join two surfaces by melting the adhesive in a fusible product with an iron.

Fusible – iron-on; any product that includes an adhesive that is activated by heating with an iron.

Paper backed fusible web – a fusible adhesive with a protective paper or silicone backing that is sold by the yard. Web is fused, paper backing side up, to one surface, paper backing is removed and then web is fused to another surface, joining the two surfaces.

Brands include:
Pellon® Wonder Under®, Dritz® Magic Fuse™, ThermO Web HeatnBond™.

Paper backed fusible web tape – precut widths of fusible web available on rolls; used for seams, hems and to fuse trims.

Brands include:
Conso® Thermo Fuse™ and Hem N Trim™, Pellon® Wonder Under®, Dritz® Iron-on Hem-n-Trim and Therm O Web Heat 'nBond™, The Warm Company, Steam A Seam® and Lite Steam-a-Seam®. (The Warm Company packages an assortment of 4 different fusible tapes in one box.)

SHIRRING TAPES

Shirring tapes – tapes that consist of a single cord or several cords inside a fabric tape casing. The tapes are fused to fabric, and when cords are pulled, the tapes create shirring or pleats in the fabric.

Single cord shirring tape – creates a single row of gathers.

Double cord shirring tape – creates narrow shirring.

ADHESIVES

Fabric glue – non-water soluble, washable glue specifically made for fabric.

Brands include:
Collins Unique-Stitch, Beacons Fabri Tac, Alene's OK to Wash-It, Crafter's Pick Fabric Glue, Delta Stitchless, Dritz Liquid Stitch, UHU Glue Works Fabric Glue.

Hot glue – comes in the form of sticks that are melted in an electric glue gun; provides a strong, long-lasting bond in items that will not be washed or dry cleaned.

Liquid fray preventative – used on raw edges of fabric to prevent raveling.

DRAPERY HARDWARE

Conventional rod – ¾" w standard metal or clear plastic rod. Also called a U-rod.

Double rod – 2 conventional rods mounted on the same brackets; used to hang 2 layers of window treatment together.

Decorative pole rod – 1¼" diameter rod made to be seen, decorative brackets and finials may be used.

Spring tension rod – ½" diameter rod fits inside window frame and requires no brackets.

Clip-on café rings – clips for hanging curtains which do not have a casing.